A Carpenter's Building, Homes for his Poems

Dear Doug

I hope you enjoy these
I wouldn't say they are poems
to hug, but there's a need
for more poetry, and your
tell stories, create scenes
and emotions I love.

poems by

Glenn D'Alessio

Finishing Line Press
Georgetown, Kentucky

A Carpenter's Building, Homes for his Poems

To my Mother, Father, daughter Rebecca, son Daniel,
and to carpenters and builders like
Bernard Nowak, Matthew Bansfield, and David Stalker

ACKNOWLEDGMENTS

I would like to thank *Borderlands*, Texas Review No. 38, 2008 for publication of
Great Blue.

Publisher: Leah Maines

Editor: Christen Kincaid

Cover Art: ~~Richard~~ John Hartman

Author Photo: Denise D'Alessio

Cover Design: Gail Heath

Printed in the USA on acid-free paper.
Order online: www.finishinglinepress.com
                also available on amazon.com

Author inquiries and mail orders:
Finishing Line Press
P. O. Box 1626
Georgetown, Kentucky 40324
U. S. A.

Table of Contents

A Captive of My Past

No longer a question of being
anyone's door mat, trash basket,
or attic space for forgotten boxes,
I crawl across linoleum
cutting slots for flashing
beneath the rafters,
dusting on my belly,
bruising ribs to keep out the rain
before building a dormer
for someone else's expansion
in the bottom of the roof
under what was a tree
bracing what will be removed,

finding stories of Buck Rogers
and Little Orphan Annie
padding the linoleum,
a captured "unicell"
having grown larger with time,
almost killing "Professor Humo,"
while the Judge's gang lures Annie
with a phony diamond,
making light of my toil
and soil I've been soaking,
a dust mop for the thoughtless,
and captive in
this fifty-year time capsule.

* plots for *Buck Rogers* and *Little Orphan Annie*
found in the August 3, 1958,   *Worcester Telegram and Gazette*
comics.

Great Blue

The blue heron
sits as if each day is new,
not moving, waiting for prey,
and the longer he stays
the smaller his wetland becomes,
roads and developments
running the shore,
his pond becoming puddle,
as he huddles
close to the thinning reeds,
not seen,
and too soon
only in our dreams.

Stars of Water

Jewels bedeck my lumber racks,
downpours beading its pipes,
pleasing my eyes
like a string of lights
brightening a cloudy day
before I leave the gems,
going back to tearing out windows,
exposing the soul of a house
on a windless day,
no rain blowing in,
the arts of carpentry no match
to draping the trees
in these stars of water.

Centrifugal Force, Opposed

The secret
to a circular saw
cutting curves
is to never back up.

Never straighten
running off, but
cut new arcs out of the old,
trusting the teeth,

and dipping the tip
a quarter-inch or less,
making multiple passes,
letting the kerf go wild!

Or all will be lost,
like being so straight
you can never go
out of your rocker.

Instead of Counting Sheep

Instead of counting sheep
I count stairs I have built—
how steep they rise
and deep their runs
making treads from rough sawn oak,

planing boards one-inch thick
twenty seconds per foot
of treads ten-inches wide,
pushing and pulling
more quickly through

to avoid blackening if they pause
in the thrum of machine,
my ear drums crumbling
like moss of sawdust
beneath my feet.

Toy Soldiers

A box of one-inch nails
fell off a stack
of rough sawn pine
on top of chest-high
saw horses; no choice
but to crawl beneath them
and into a tall grass forest
of German and American
infantry on patrol,
soon to battle
under a strategic railroad trestle
army engineers are
setting charges on,
so I better watch my head
from falling timbers
in the explosions,
like other soldiers exposed,
until my partner wonders
why it takes me so long
to pick up a few dozen tiny
nails scouting in the brush,
since he's oblivious to WW II.

Dead Strength

A bundle of asphalt shingles,
or a fifty pound sack of potatoes
are dead loads
with no crisp leverage,
only limp to lift,

unlike my uncle's drill press
with steel cylinder and spindle,
inflexibly rigid,
I attempt to move its table to thirty-six degrees
for cable rail holes to be drilled in cedar posts.

Needing to loosen a bolt
larger than one-inch in diameter,
prudent, I move the drill bit
away from where my hand may slip,
understanding how tight

my one-armed Uncle Wes
must have tightened it
twenty-two years ago,
almost not budging
with my shiny crescent wrench.

I feel my uncle's
dead strength stored for so long
give way, as if he has something to say:
welder's beads,
and many more nuts to crack.

At the Sterling Ice Cream Shop

They looked like flies,
there were so many Harleys
buzzing around the
blacktop parking lot, making
time for hot dogs and cigarettes.

Outside the Masonic Home

The grounds keeper
straddles an all-terrain-vehicle,
taming the sidewalk,
smoking a stogie,
spraying stonewalls,
circling pesticide soaked fingers
around his cigar,
drawing deeply,
killing weeds,
happy with his detail
on a cloudless day
before the weeds inside him
take seed.

The Termite Man

At least there isn't a giant termite
atop his bright orange truck.
Sometimes the albinos
go unseen in the dark

of the neighbor's house
on a listless day in July
on Lake Wickaboag
where poisons mustn't leach.

He introduces me to his work
where I sit next door
on a plank over horses,
resting from construction.

"I'm going to be fumigating termites"
he cordially warns.
But the news to me is like cordite and lead
spreading through vectors with a sledge.

He thinks it's aftershave,
"Safer than botanicals
we use on our bodies,
and it's biodegradable!"

'Degradeable speech' I muse,
going to high ground,
up two streets,
and eat lunch.

Upon my return, job done, he greets me
while eating in his pickup, windows down,
no masks up, since his company
doesn't want to alarm the public.

Whereupon, he concludes,
"I don't need calls about my harmless fog."
A kid on a bicycle waves.
I pray for rain.

The Worst and the Best of Views

In the newest spot off of Long Hill Road
the pumpkins are too symmetrically spaced for nature,
mulch machined and dyed an unnatural sheen,
corn stalks a march of hydras for Halloween.

The view of the hill from the river
brown and barren in fall,
inlayed with a golden oak's glory,
and a gory gash for the white mansion

evenly overlaying an autumn display
on the bulldozer's slash into oxides,
and the woodsman's cut yielding the best
panorama of the Quaboag River.

In the Bushes

Playing hide-and-seek
in the laurel and boxwood,
will the yellow jackets
or purple dragon flies find me,

fixing wooden skirts
with me being it,
and the sun and wind
seekers too.

Not Knowing an End Grain from a Knot Hole

I told them
not to use the same grains
to screw together our window frames
and despite taking pains
to explain what I meant
I suspect they had no clue
to how many years of a tree
we were using.

Against the Grain

"Only speak if spoken to"
was not how I
brought up my children,
yet in old age I must be silent,
the knot in the log I'm splitting
grown over, unseen,
excessive blows
almost ineffective,

when another log
is only worth burning
since the carpenter ants' hole
indicates there's something left,
unlike the pith of a whiter looking log,
yet grubs eating there
mean it's not all whipped cream
the way anything I say is perceived,

not all pieces as easy as red oak to split;
one baby born in Singapore
having two heads and necks,
twice the cry, and even two spines,
cannot be untwined,
like when everyone is angry
there is no gain
to following the grain.

Digging Sono Tube Holes

Like wooly aldegids
or pine bark borers
who never tire of eating feasts,

they bring picks and shovels,
and froth at the start of their holes,
bringing grub hoes, and post hole diggers;

bars, and longer bars and pipes;
malls, hatchets, and machetes for roots,
so I suppose they are going to have

a smorgasborg of tubers and rocks
cooked in hardpan and topsoil,
before mixing concrete

and pouring it down holes,
Dan and Tim so well equipped
they almost forget what the job is.

Reusing Galaxies of Judy's

Patching a fieldstone foundation
willow roots pulled out
is one of those nebulas things—
which galaxy of rocks
do you start with,

from how many light years away,
in five dimensions, black holes,
or antimatter, with sand-mix cement
and small stones finding homes
in what becomes concrete,

re-using temporary stair treads,
now for form boards, and reusing
large fieldstones near the top,
until we have the rebirth of a galaxy
rising up from the earth.

The Ramshackle House that's Not Unattractive

You are easy to smile
and easy to laugh,
so fit for a simile

like ventilation baffles
in the eves of an attic
flapping in the wind,

and chuckle at birds
singing in the soffits
poor carpenters are to fix

with toothpicks for perches
trying to coax critters out of their homes,
like upside down bats from the ridge boards,

as if a hoard of people
is better than birds and bats,
or squirrels that the carpenter knows

since they talk about architecture
and the historical preservation
of their nests in nooks and rookeries,

so he lets them go,
and writes a poem for you instead,
knowing you'll laugh.

Terrible News

Green screws and black phosphorous
threads that are coarse
have additional ceramics to resist corrosion
from yellow pine treated with copper
to kill microbes and rot,

high tech ring shank nails
of stainless steel for cedar
that bleeds, being put away,
last year's job on hold
when we're only a year older,

yet carpentry and fasteners
suddenly worth little,
like boxes of eight-penny
galvanized deck nails
not worth a nickel,

and stainless steel washers—
left over clutter being sorted,
no longer worried about whose fasteners these are,
no longer keeping them out in case I return to fix
some more holes in his house,

for the holes in his stomach
are beyond repair,
and the masses inside of him
desperately need
unfastening.

Peanut

Peanut, not the most flattering
nickname for a shop teacher,
but his bald head was polished
like our year long projects
were supposed to be,

mine a half-inch thick
by three-inch wide board
eighteen-inches high,
with three maple leaf shapes glued on
after being cut in the band saw,

meant to hold photos
and our parent's affections,
all our projects identically shaped
and first mechanically drawn,
only different when polished

after days of hand sanding,
and more days of hand sanding,
when I don't think I ever saw
my father or grandfather,
both union carpenters, ever sanding,

so I thought I knew a thing or two
more than boring hobby work,
yet now that I'm older than when
my father and grandfather retired,
I am still working

and sanding some custom cabinets
I'm building, even though
I still can't stand sanding,
I try to sand the oak
smoother than Peanut's waxy head was,

since any scratch marks not seen before,
show up too late once stain is applied,
and too late then to remake everything
if my work looks like an un-husked peanut
covered in hairy roots,

remembering the B I received
for a lack luster effort
that would become F
in the real world
of my customer's cabinets.

Planing Red Oak

A ruby rich
deep throated thrum
from the diamond hard oak
leaves unsound knots
dancing in vibrations
out of their holes,

while powder post beetle bores
are planing away, when shallow enough,
moving fifty-feet per hour,
or at a rate of creep
less than one-foot per minute,
pushing boards with knees

and hands in gloves, reading
"Keep Clothes and Fingers
Away From Machinery"
in red, but fingers in leather
measure more than
one-inch settings are turned to,

vibrations losing screws
and wing nuts
like malevolent hands
are unscrewing them,
thus securing housings
and guards with tape,

just keeping them from being lost
when not absolutely necessary
for marrying rollers and knives
to the smoothest surfaces sliced,
as if Pinocchio's nose
could be smooth as glass,

some of the wood smelling
like vanilla cakes baking,
with other boards astringent
like dirty toenails, but
where did these trees grow
to be so maligned

and lined straight
away from organic shapes,
taking out cups
and curves,
when turning the screw
down one-quarter at a time,

respirator popping
by keeping fine dust
out of one's lungs,
drops of vapor splashing
temperatures falling
pulverized dust exploding

when trees are dormant
in cold seasons like these,
boards sounding deep and slow
the wider they are,
sawdust accumulating
for future use as humus,

narrow boards almost
self-feeding into the machine,
not much for microbes
in a more restrained music
keeping wood
to different sides of the planer

reducing heat of friction,
even in the cold
where any moisture
in wood is frozen,
letting knives
slice more easily

like in the first passes
of rough-sawn boards,
less of their flesh
enmeshed in the machine,
cold steel of no appeal
to the feelings of wood

meeting a machine
surreal to the carpenter,
not revealing what trees think
when their passing boards
do not squeal in the
throws of their movements,

throats too deep
for the carpenter
to contemplate,
and it is too late
for good conscience
to hear what they say,

listening to them a sacrilege
to the worship of efficiency,
efficiency being
how fast trees fall
and how fast their sap bleeds out
before they're peeled and sawn,

of no concern
when the forest floor
and soils wash away,
and no concern for the
hydrocarbons strip-mined
so the machine can whine

because the wider
and smoother a board,
the lower its words
until indecipherable
to the wood worker
more attuned

to machine bearings
staying cool,
avoiding their screech,
his philosophy being
for the gloss and grain
of the surface,

and not for what's lost
like rain in the forest,
or when it comes too hard,
pebbles and soil screaming
when sweeping into the stream
that loses its voice

in loose deposits of silt
while saplings in the field
wilt or are stripped by deer
who follow humans
who have proven ruinous
to past civilizations

when the carpenter plies his trade
as long as there are trees,
worshiping them in his way
for furniture and houses
with things like floors and roofs
still made of wood in New England

where trees still grow
and the hum of a
one-by-six board of red oak
has a thrum like its roots
had been deep and mellow
until squeaking into the machine

and having all this to say
as boards sway
between rollers and knives,
singing in their slide,
with the tightest knots
bringing out the throatiest timber

of the richest notes
from the lowest pipe organ
with the density
of so many growth rings
the carpenter groans,
small atonement

for all he has done,
when he believes
there is so much more to come;
edging and milling the pieces,
making cabinets and doors
as long as resources last,

amassing piles of boards;
one-by-eights vibrating
like a grizzlies's chest
to those entering his forest,
so the carpenter should
believe these challenges

by respecting the wood
and all his ancestors
who worked it before,
and he should love
all flora and fauna
that formerly flourished

and stood within the forest,
and not fall for the allure
of a planer making boards
for those who can afford them
with roads through the forests
where more tools may be moved,

so don't let 60 cycles and 15 amps
at 120 volts for the motor
jolt the life out of trees,
but let fairy tales continue
to come from the woods
and be told about the hold

trees have on imagination,
and heed what boards say they need,
that there is a deeper purpose in life
than to become the seat for a
fat man's bottom, when sometimes
red oak smells like strawberries

when being carved smooth
and deprived of life,
so do the right thing,
leave us alone, and stop
shamelessly feeding your
plunder into the planer.

Before He Comes

Hot cross buns,
Belgium block, or bricks;
what kind of mix do you want;

not too soupy,
and not too thick
that sets up quick;

the lead, like icing,
malleable enough
to flash away water

from the chimney's peak
where we listen
to Christmas bells,

rebuilding it for Saint Nick
on a beautiful day, only one
month before he comes.

Yesterday's Exacting Details,

The kind still with me, being stimulated in the morning, with details
kindly grinding me into the reddish brown earth beneath the barn,
composted boards chiffon to the touch, mingled with tingling grains
of sawdust bedding, a springing manure mattress surrounding gigantic
posts sprouting from granite peers between broad fieldstone walls
exposed on top by powder post beetles and more active forces of rainwater
microbes, finished by pry bars, arms, and fingers grinning with delight

digging into mortises—more distinct as empty shapes, absence of bulk
folding over the last checkered facet of the eight-by-eight sill,
still, from all its rolling motion over years of decay,
praying we would respect hundreds of years of introspection
workers passed on for centuries, placing each mortise patiently,
now gone by the final gnawing of our palms,
scarcely disturbing a century-and-a-half's fieldstone face

pointed on top now by the sun, when earlier, sound like a gun shot
was not the barn's back, as we synchronously cranked our jacks
atop twin pressure treated posts almost twinning around each other
in their intricate ballet, boosting the corner of the formidable
feldspar based behemoth of an extinct species of chestnut
bringing all guests luck with one horseshoe near a door,
as I mused, how will we move the new sixteen-foot eight-by-eight

with odds and ends of only three men, until attaching pipe clamps
underneath, one-quarter from the end for two of us to hoist two-thirds
of the weight, while I took the diminished freight of the ship-lapped end,
our load equitably dispersed with one word left to express,
let's "christen" her with a beer bottle, though I do not drink,
beginning to think we could move this monster into place,
expecting it to fit into the same barn's groove that stood the test of time

until its former owner sold the gable end's boards to an entrepreneur—
a snake oil salesman's offer, "being too good to refuse," what the heck if
the rain gets it wet? The black barn boards worth gold, were lost through

fraud, then like garbage to the owner, for ten years not re-siding, finally
deciding to let me preserve the most monolithic side reaching for the sky,
where I thought I'd die, thirty-five feet high, balanced on staging planks
straddling posts in and out of the barn, with diagonals angling down

from closer to the peak, providing counter thrust to our corporal trust,
clinging to a platform as we climbed out of the barn,
like hammer beating bats doing that siding job five years ago,
time giving it a little patina, with us distributing the weight
of our latest challenge, chinking the cracks beneath this big beam—
installed, called a sill, with us wanting it to remain still,
instilled with confidence "we'll get it right"

while Dave leaned lightly on my peavey—a logger's tool,
rolling the girth of the sill ever so slightly
as the latest owner, an archeologist, looked for arrow head stones
and axe flinted ones, chinking and sledging them in
on top of the foundation's ledge, hedging our wedges between
blue green crumbling sandstones and mica speckled igneous rocks,
greeting our ingenious leverage with little more than indifference, as we

eased the barn's load onto the sill that appeared to be hardly squeezed,
and we were thrilled by how easy this was done, having finished the job
mostly in the dark, feeling like larks without pressure on our minds
while the barn was propped precariously on jacks.
Instead, we stopped holding our breaths, conscious of the cold fresh air
and stars on far journeys lighting faint fields and forest,
from our perspective pleased with the ease and clarity,

nay, satisfied with the charity of the elements—
not attacking the exacting details of brute force and finesse,
not overshooting the capacity of our muscles and tendons
tending the temple of our endeavor, not for us to worship forever, but
expecting the barn to outlast our life spans, with its dirt welcome in our
eyes, the next day reminding us of how kind it has been to withstand the
weather, and our latest meddling, letting us pet the cow stanchions,

leaving them for their ambiance, our archeologist said,
marveling at where they rubbed their heads,
and I imagined one of their Holstein hairs was wedged
into one sliver of wood, integrally part of the structure,
propping up our delight with life,
full of strife cutting like a knife sometimes,
but not for this day and brightly lit night.

Joining Boards

Like a perfume
that does not choose the direction it travels,
that cannot be straight or crooked, kept out or kept.
(Jane Hirshfield)

Time to write is not right
when taking time from time to work
crooked oak to be straightened
patiently but fast,
skillfully cutting out knots
and doubts about clearness
for something like the purity of perfume
metered and rhymed to defy the abstraction
of a consistent flavor named "Seduction"
of a rose exposed to your nose
as more than a rose of a nose
seeking subtle fragrances
until the oak is cut,
expecting the saw's fence cannot slip,
like taking a sip of time
and expecting the clamps
are strong enough to straighten
the iron will of the red oak
that in the past twisted in the sun
and is a memory that lasts,
defying the abstraction
of getting work done in time
when hoping the oak will smell
like strawberries again,
and that the milk glue
will not be confusing
like almonds plus pine nuts
welding boards together
with egg yokes in the mix,
not creating "Seduction,"

but sides and shelves
to hold spices and herbs
more like verbs that keep running
beyond time, kept out, or kept,
as entropy tosses them ever more faintly
to where they seem lost,
so maybe waiting for poetry and Godot
before starting the work
will leave things imagined
more concentrated,
while piles of wood rest
before being dressed for purposes
less mighty than the lives they're from,
like re-purposing lines from
Jane Hirschfield's, "Like Two
Negative Numbers Multiplied by Rain"
we cannot define, but easily rhyme.

Glenn D'Alessio lives with his wife and son in West Brookfield, Massachusetts. There, he still sometimes gets to enjoy framing rafters and a few stairs as a carpenter; in-between poetry and flute playing in jazz and concert bands, while sometimes teaching college courses about energy, energy conservation, and green building.

His poetry seems to hold more energy than the calories required to write it. There's no such thing as a perpetual motion machine. The 2nd Law of Thermodynamics, really of entropy and of spreading waste, cannot be avoided. Early in his brief Carpenter's Union days of work, brain cells were lost while spreading cut-back glue for floor tiles at Westbury State College, and concrete slabs were swept by hand on his knees. Later, framing houses and barns in New England left little energy for literary pursuits. For years he would write poetry about many things, but when being exhausted from doing carpentry he was unable to use it as a theme. Like the memory of an apple picking ladder's rungs on Robert Frost's feet, Glenn could feel little other than the imprint of tools and repetitive labor upon his muscles at night. Nor could he often see the grace of the forest for the trees milled into boards being used when he was under the gun of time and production over craftsmanship. Yet, his poem, "Great Blue," reflects a growing concern for the consequences of suburban sprawl. Later he learned that for our built environment to endure it must include not only expert joinery but beauty.

While wanting to please carpenters like his father, grandfather, and dead ancestors (whose work ranged from the Suez Canal, to a secret US Air Force base on Baffin Island in the Arctic) his attitude seemed like Feng shui. But when his father asked, "What good is your poetry," he had no answer. Now he would say, without poetry he could not be a carpenter. He also reflects about the ripple effects and consequences of building without green practices. The bird pavilion on the cover of this, his second book published by Finishing Line Press, was commissioned and designed by Gail Heath, with Glenn's help and carpentry. It joins nature in an urban setting. As a shelter and sanctuary, bird songs and the flapping of wings help amalgamate music, building, and poetry. In turn, the secret lives, and embodied energy of trees and plants are brought to life through John Hartman's infrared photograph of the bird pavilion that may someday provide more, "Homes for His Poems."

CPSIA information can be obtained
at www.ICGtesting.com
Printed in the USA
BVOW08s2259290117
474731BV00001B/4/P

9 781635 341157